God Loves You

for Mathijs and Cosima

God Loves You

Kathryn Maris

SEREN

Seren is the book imprint of
Poetry Wales Press Ltd.
57 Nolton Street, Bridgend, Wales, CF31 3AE
www.serenbooks.com
Facebook:facebook.com/SerenBooks
Twitter: @SerenBooks

The right of Kathryn Maris to be identified as
the author of this work has been asserted in accordance
with the Copyright, Designs and Patents Act, 1988.

ISBN: 978-1-78172-035-6
Kindle ISBN: 078-1-78172-037-0
e-book ISBN: 987-1-78172-036-3

A CIP record for this title is available from the British Library.

The publisher acknowledges the financial assistance of the Welsh Books Council.

Cover art:
Printed in Bembo by Berforts Group, Stevenage.

Table of Contents

I
What Will the Neighbours Think?

II
God Loves You

III
Praise Him

Crow realised God loved him –
Otherwise he would have dropped dead
So that was proved.
                  – Ted Hughes

I
What Will the Neighbours Think?

Is it nothing to you, all ye that pass by?
— Lamentations 1:12

What Will Happen to the Neighbours
When the Earth Floods?

In the foreground there is an isolated flat slab of rock on which some helpless humans have taken refuge just at the moment when the flood is welling nearer and is about to cover them.

    — Goethe on Jacob More's painting 'The Deluge'

Sometimes I mistake Noah for God, but sometimes I mistake God for no one.

I mistake Noah for God because even in his arms I'm abandoned.

From my High Ground you can see my neighbours, but it's hard to look.

So here are my glasses.

Is that a raft? Because I think it's a boatman who hangs his head in the storm.

But is that a raft or is it a rock? Could it be one rock lower than Ararat?

I love my neighbours and I think God would love me for this.

But I covet my neighbours too, and God might proscribe this if he had laws.

Look at my neighbours with nothing to covet. Now see the container I live in with too much to hold.

There are my neighbours; here's my container.

Here's me, the doves, the griffins, the dogs, the bears, the boys, and my man who can look like God when the weather's not clear.

And the weather is unclear a lot.

I remind him of the neighbours, but he says, 'Look. I don't want to be reminded of the neighbours.'

I can be distant with him, but I feel affection when he eats.

When he eats, he bows his head like that boatman who probably isn't a boatman but a neighbour pressing against the weather on almost the last land in the world.

The Witch and Macduff Exit
My Neighbour's House

My neighbour was a bitch
in Stoppard, a witch
in Shakespeare, a lawyer
on *The Bill*,
but she's 'herself'
when she's over the wall
with her daughter,
my favourite child
next to my own,
who are friends with her one day
and not the next,
like when my son
accused her of stealing
a Gameboy cartridge,
and my daughter repeated
an awful thing
I say about the English,
that they're the rudest people
on the planet.
But as for my neighbour:
I smile through tears
when she and her daughter
are over the wall
playing together
and I'm watching
from a location
akin to
a box seat.
She might have
a box seat too –
my other neighbour
definitely does
because she knows
everything I do.
All the world's a stage

and all the neighbours
merely players
with their exits,
like the one my neighbour made
with Macduff
in the middle of the day,
a little too happy –
and I thought I knew the plot.
Every tear
I shed for her
is – what's that called? –
anagnorisis,
or just plain *catharsis*,
or moving on
from Aristotle,
there's always Freud,
who'd call this 'projection'.
Our houses sit
in a row
all of them built
in the fashion of their time,
and you could make the mistake
of calling them
identical.
So when my neighbour
is with her daughter,
I try to grasp
her motivation,
dry my tears,
stand up straight,
enter the room
with the television,
smile and project,
'It's a lovely day!
Let's go out to the garden,
and have a play.'

Why I Will Gladly Take Your Man Away

Because there is time
and because I can claim Him and then declaim
to you, 'I know not what I do,'
and because I've settled for impotence,
while you have omnipotence,

if you've got God, then watch Him hard
because I will take Him if I can
and I know that I can because I have heard
He loves me as much as He loves you,
and because you have God and I have no one

but a ladder, which I drag to the beach
and drag in the rain
and which wobbles in the wind
so I can place it in the right place
to climb to Him in His big home.

My mother preaches: *Marry up!*
All's fair in love and God, girl, so take Him
and keep Him, and ask that He keep you
for Himself, who can provide.
Just ask, and I tell you − you'll receive!

Hilary Has Left the Building,
Unless She Hasn't

Hilary did something to her house:
no one knows exactly *what*
she did, but it is wrecked
and no one can enter for fear
of the whole thing collapsing.

The firemen stood outside her door
for a few solid days
but they left to save another house
on which they could use their hatchets –
and that had a better outcome.

Her parents and friends have knocked
at the door gingerly,
as have employees of the council,
and even a devious estate agent
who saw a plot of land at the ready.

I, too, knocked,
questioning her, as a teacher must,
and though it had always been in her nature
to give me the correct answers,
this time there was nothing.

The matter remains to this day:
if she is still in the house
there can be no hasty decisions;
but if she has left the house
the structure can be razed without regret.

Kill a Tree, Kill Me

My husband, whom I loved enough to live
in any country with, warned me against
his own, the Netherlands, because he sensed
my utopian preconceptions were naïve.
I thought the Dutch were unremonstrative
and green, were droll, couldn't be influenced,
rode bikes. He claimed my views were unbalanced,
and furthermore he'd be uncooperative
if I attempted bicycling. It turned
out that we moved to neutral ground: a house
near Paddington. A fig tree on the side
grew big after ten years. So I discerned
him with his saw last week, and near him was
a brand new bike he'd bought for me to ride.

This Is a Confessional Poem

I am guilty of so much destruction it hardly matters
anymore. There are so many thank-you notes I never wrote
that sometimes I'm relieved by the deaths of would-be
recipients, so I can finally let go of the shame.
I was awful to someone who was attached to the phrase
'social polish', as though she'd acquire it through repetition.
I took an overdose at a child's 6th birthday party.
I was born in a country which some have called
The Big Satan. I abandoned the country for one
that is called The Little Satan. I wished ill on a woman
who has known me for years and yet never remembers
who I am – and now she's involved in a public scandal.
I have been at parties where I was boring.
I have been at parties where I was deadly boring.
I have worn the wrong clothes to sacraments, not
for lack of outfits, but for a temporary failure of taste.
I'm a terrible, terrible liar, and everything I say is full of
misrepresentation. I once knew a very sweet girl
who stabbed herself in the abdomen 7 times.
She believed she was evil and thought 7 was a holy number.
Besides that she was sane, and told me her tale
out of kindness – because guilt recognises guilt,
the way a mother can identify her own child.
I met her in a class called 'Poetry Therapy'
in which the assignment was to complete this statement:
When one door closes, another opens.
I wrote *At the end of my suffering there was a door,*
making me guilty of both plagiarism and lack of imagination.
I was the vortex of suffering: present, future and retroactive
suffering. The girl tried to absolve me.
'Don't be Jesus,' she said. 'There are enough around here.'
I know I should thank her if she's alive,
but I also know it's unlikely I'll rise to the task.

Darling, Would You Please
Pick up those Books?

How many times do I have to say
get rid of the books off the goddamn floor
do you have any idea how it feels
to step over books you wrote about *her*
bloody hell you sadist what kind of man
are you all day long those fucking books

in my way for 3 years your *acclaimed* books
tell me now what do you have to say
for yourself you think you're such a man
silent brooding pondering at the floor
pretending you're bored when I mention *her*
fine change the subject ask 'Do I feel

like I need more medication' NO I don't *feel
like I need more medication* it's the books
don't you see don't you see it's *her*
why don't you listen to anything I say
and for God's sake books on the floor
are a *safety hazard* remember that man

from Cork who nearly died fine that man
fell over a hurley not a book but I don't feel
you're getting the point the point is that a floor
is not an intelligent place for books
books *I* have to see and books that say
exactly where and how you shagged her

what shirt she wore before you shagged her
I can write a book too about some man
better still about *you* I can say
something to *demonize* you how would you feel
about *that* ha ha why don't I write a book
about how I *hoover your sodding floor*

and how you've *never once* hoovered your floor
why can't I be a muse why can't I be a 'her'
what does one have to do to be in a book
around here do I have to be *dead* for a man
to write me a poem how do you think it feels
to be non-muse material can't you say

you feel for me what you felt for her
can't you say I'm better than that woman
can't you get those books off the floor?

Will You Be My Friend, Kate Moss?

My daughter's in your daughter's ballet class.
I sat beside you at the Christmas show?
I really loved the outfit you had on!
Three years ago I tried to emulate
your look in *Grazia*: you can't believe
how hard it was to find some knee-high boots,
a tunic-dress, and earrings just like yours.
The icon of my generation, you
were motivation when we exercised.
You were The Waif – that's what we aimed to be –
and yet it's so unfair you got the blame
for all that teenage anorexia.
We'd never look like you no matter what:
I saw that when you walked into the class
(your daughter was ecstatic, by the way!)
your terrifying cheekbones mocking mine.
The line 'Alas, poor Yorick!' struck me then:
your head could easily be on Hamlet's palm!
And speaking of: I heard your friend Jude Law
is in New York reprising Hamlet at
the Broadhurst Theatre on 44th.
I miss New York – I wish that we could go.
I have this friend, Nuar, I'm sure you'd love:
she's smarter than the two of us combined,
and stunning, too, and has two little girls.
At Yaddo, where we met, she'd quote Foucault
and Nietzsche on the buffet line. She held
my hand one creepy night when we got lost
around the lake beside her studio.
I really miss Nuar, and Suki too,
whose sense of style is on a par with yours.
Let's all go out one night! I'll do my best
to stick with you despite the fact that I'm
a hypochondriac and petrified
of class A drugs. We have so many things
in common, like you're pretty much my age;
we share initials; the circumference of

our thighs is basically the same. (I checked.)
I also saw you surreptitiously
admire my silver space-age dress! You did!
Now that my daughter's been moved up a grade
will this be *adios amigo*, Kate?
She's not disconsolate about the change
but then she's at the age where all you say
is 'will you be my friend.' Remember that?

I Told No One for as Long as Possible

I had a terrible dream
my daughter was dead.
In a refrigerator.
At the morgue.

My daughter was dead.
I told no one.
She was at the morgue.
It couldn't be true.

I told no one
for six weeks,
so it wouldn't be true
my daughter was dead.

For six weeks
the morgue rang.
'Your daughter is dead.
Come take her away.'

The morgue rang
again and again:
'Come take her away!'
I left her there.

Again and again
I avoided friends.
I left her there,
afraid I'd crack.

I avoided friends
but I went to work.
And then I cracked.
I told the boss

when I went to work,
'My daughter is dead.'
I looked at his face,
his busy eyes.

'Onze dochter is dood!'
I cried to her father.
'Her Byzantine eyes
looked into mine – '

I cried to her father
in my sleep.
He said, 'Look at me.
It was a terrible dream.'

On Returning a Child to Her Mother at the Natural History Museum

Hello, my name is Kathryn and I've come
here to return your daughter, Emily.
She told me you'd suggested that she look
around upstairs in 'Earthquakes and Volcanoes,'
then meet you and her brothers in the shop.
You know that escalator leading to
the orb? It's very long and only goes
one way, you can't turn round. She asked me if
I knew the way back down and would we come
with her into the earthquake simulator –
that reproduction of the grocery shop
in Kobe, where you see the customers
get thrown around with Kirin beer and soy
sauce, things like that. She told us stuff about
your family. Apparently you had
a baby yesterday! That can't be right:
you're sitting here without one and my God
your stomach's flat! She also said she'd had
an operation in the hospital
while you were giving birth one floor below.
I know, I know: kids lie and get confused,
mine do that too. She talks a lot. She's fat.
She may not be an easy child to love.
I liked her, though. I liked her very much,
and having her was great, the only time
all day my daughter hasn't asked me for
a dog! We got downstairs and funnily
enough we found your middle son. He ran
to us upset and asked us where you were.
But here you are – exactly where you said –
the shop! Don't worry: I don't ever judge
a mother. Look at me: my daughter drank
the Calpol I left out when she was two;
I gave my kids Hundreds and Thousands once
for dinner while I lay down on the floor,
a wreck. I know you well! Here's Emily.

I Imagine We Will Be Neighbours in Hell

*...in Hell there is a gray tulip that grows without any sun. It reminds
me of everything I failed at,*

and I water it carefully.
— Sarah Manguso

We couldn't be sisters, so let's be neighbours.
You can water your stone plant
and I'll climb stairs that hang in my vacant world.
We'll know our neighbours; we just won't know
they *are* our neighbours. Hell could be that:
ignorance of the proximity of our neighbours.

You'll weep for your plant, but sadder still:
I'll believe in what I do. And sadder still:
we'll never know that thin walls hide
the other neighbours – the men who loved us
then sent us to hell
for lacking souls even in the world.

One floor above, someone who envied our youth
we didn't think was youth, or success
that was really grief, will perform an everlasting tap dance
partly to annoy but mostly because she has no choice.
If I cared or even owned a broom, I could pound at the ceiling
and shout: *Come down and love the misery of company!*

II
God Loves You

Nobody Is Not Loved
   – placard on a council estate near Elephant and Castle

Always hoped that I'd be an apostle
knew that I would make it if I tried.
Then when I retire
I can write the Gospels
So they'll all talk about me when I've died.
   – Jesus Christ Superstar

God Loves You

1. God's image was in the mirror and God's image was my grief. And lo, I knew I was not loved by Him and wept. And I knew shame. For though I was young, I was not young enough to weep in the face of the Lord who made me.

2. In sorrow, I set out. I prayed that God might look on me in my search for signs of love in His great world.

3. The first sign was clear: the call from Tom, Tom-Who-Loves-Me-Not. When he spoke unto me, he said three times, 'I love you,' and I knew it was He, for Tom is like God in sound and in grace. And that was a strong sign.

4. On the second day, there were finches in the air. I saw with my own eyes this flock yield the form of a heart before me.

5. The next sign, too, was full of meaning. It was a sign. And it was revealed to me thus: the Damut Estate. And in that name I read these words: *'Deus te amat.'*

6. On the road there was a child who pressed into my palm a yo-yo, where it was written: 'God loves you.' And I thanked the child, held him and wept, for he was righteous, and he was called Matthew. But still I was unloved.

7. For if God is in the mirror, and if God is the mirror of our world, then the signs will be false, for the world will reverse what God has shown me.

It Was a Gift from God

1. And the Lord said 'Go to the woman who toils in the grove and give her this box.' And the angel asked not what was in the box, but delivered it to the woman.

2. The woman knew the ways of the Lord, so when she saw that the box was full of grief, she was not afraid.

3. God said 'Take this grief, for it belonged to the One Who Came Before You, and she can bear it no longer. Take it to the East, as far as the next land.'

4. The woman did as God bid, but a soldier saw what she carried and threw her before the King.

5. The King asked 'Why have you dishonoured our land with your beast?' She replied, 'It is not a beast, but a burden, and the Lord hath made *me* the beast of this burden.' The King was angry and said, 'Behold again the contents of your box!' She looked again and lo there was a beast where before there was none. For this she was locked away.

6. She prayed and the Lord was merciful. 'You were burdened with a beast and now you are captive like the beast. Go to the farthest sea and the beast will follow you, and there he will leave you forever.'

7. So the lord sent an angel to open the prison door and it came to pass that the woman was followed to the sea by the beast who, when it was night, fled to the dunes and withdrew from this world.

The Devil Got into Her

1. The woman appealed to the Doctor, for she could not be cured. The Doctor had the likeness of the Lord, and the Lord spoke through him: 'You are overcome by a demon. When it is slain, it will harm you no longer.'

2. The woman asked how the demon should be slain, and the Doctor said there was a man but that she must be the one to find him.

3. The woman found a man who said he could slay the demon, but he did not, for he was a demon himself and full of trickery. So the woman slew the man and was not punished, for the King of the land was glad to be rid of him.

4. She returned to the Doctor and told of her failure. 'Tell me the name of this demon that has made me its home.' But this he would not reveal.

5. So again she set out. An angel took the form of a crone and said, 'Find the man in the west whose name is "Slay."'

6. So the woman found that man and he said to her, 'God hath forbidden me to rid you of this demon. But in the city to the east there is a man who can help you.' And he told her where to find him.

7. The man in the east was kind, so the woman came to live with him. But he was kind to the demon too, for he did not kill it, but placed it in a box. And the woman was healed, but still she feared the demon and viewed the box askance.

Why

Before I was God
as you know Him to be
I liked to sit
on my quark bench
and stretch my legs,
take in the void,
have a snooze
then wake and sketch
plans for the future.

There was no time
and then there was –
too much time –
and as I have eyes
on the back of my head
I saw it all:
the beginning, the end,
and all the carnage
in between.

When I sat on the bench
I used to like
looking at
a pagoda I made
from the finest wood
from the first tree
that would make no sound
when it hit the earth
in an earless time.

And then one day
I was disturbed
by a sound
that was a word
like 'I' or 'sky'

(it wasn't clear)
and I looked to find
there was a man
in my pagoda!

I could only conclude
his word was 'why':
he repeated himself
and had no legs
and probably was
sorry for himself,
but it was hard to hear
and harder to see
from my preferred distance.

I saw him better
with binoculars,
but had forgotten his name
and the era of his suffering
and where he was from –
then or now –
though it's all the same,
and they all say 'why' –
it's the Question of the Day.

I know I could have
banished him
but I let him stay
for he gave me ideas
and though I didn't
sleep as well,
my dreams were more vivid,
I switched on the light,
and my sketches became great.

Doubting Thomas

Call me Infidel, or just call me Tom.
Call me handsome, call me cold, call me bitter, call me cad,
call me No-Better-Than-Judas-Iscariot,
call me bachelor, call me saint, call me numb.

I was abused, I was married, I took pills, I was left,
I was in love, I was a liar, I was a drunk, I was in debt,
I wrote a book, I had some fame, then I was dead,
till I was saved, I slept around, I was too young, I was bereft.

You are good, you are beautiful, you are kind, you forgive,
you are loving, you are smart, you're adored and you are brave.

There's no one else. It isn't you. I'm circumspect. I'm full of doubt.
It wouldn't work. We're not alike. I don't know what I want.

Call me weak, call me ingrate, call me 'once bitten, twice shy.'
Call me anything, but please don't say I make you want to die.

Lord Forgive Me

Kyrie eleison! I said it in the pub.
I said it to my bitter then I said
it to my heart, with nothing not to dread:
my sins were great: I drank there with my love.

Kyrie iesu christe, God above
and me below, drinking at the Hog's Head.
'So. Will you love me better when I'm dead?'
He knew it was a joke, but didn't laugh

just turned away to look at the TV.
(Arsenal was playing Everton.)
Another man was fixed upon the game

and held his hands together on his knee
and chanted and rebuked. But not my man,
who recognizes neither loss nor blame.

Last Supper

I asked for liver as it was the closest thing to poison.
He cooked it robotically in the scratched Teflon pan.
I sat at the table like the good girl I'd mainly been.

I tried to eat the liver but was ill with bile of my own.
He ate the liver and was quiet until it was done.

Then he said he was sick of being cast as a demon,
that I'd asked too many questions that resembled accusation,
and did I know I have a limitless need for affirmation.

I had things of my own to say, but why say them.
I thought of a cad whose headstone reads *Resurgam*
and how it's like a perverse joke

and how it must be easy to be a man who can say *Resurgam*
over a death sentence, a flame or a Teflon pan –
whereas I could hardly rise from the table again.

My Father Who Art in Heaven

My father, who art in heaven,
sits under an umbrella that is his firmament.
The umbrella drifts when the wind blows
and is not much of a shelter to anyone
but him. He has kept the family under it.
He would like to keep the world under it,
and though the world is not under it,
he thinks it is, and is happy to think it.
And he's happy. He's happy when he's God, and God
is what he is when he's under his umbrella.
But when it drifts, or when he turns
it around so it's a walking stick to lean on,
he isn't God at all, but we say
he is and thank him for protecting us –
and the rest of the world too – who kneel
under trees that bow to him in the rain
and feed him fruit and fan him with their leaves
in a show of our appreciation.

Knowledge is a Good Thing

My mind is open,
so the devil can get in.

We speak in the rhythm
of catechism.

'Look at this.'
'But it is *His*.'

'What's his is yours.
Look in the drawers.'

'I'm forbidden
to know what's in them.'

'You're his wife.
Dig up his life.'

'Will I despair
at what's in there?'

'Better to know
than be in limbo.'

'That may be,
but remember the tree?'

'The world was built
on sin and guilt.'

'If that's true
it's thanks to you.'

★

He was victorious
for I was curious.

And there was no pardon
in the garden

where I sat
till He came back.

Variations on Melissanthi's *Atonement*

1. Atonement

Every time I sinned a door half opened and the Angels
who never found me virtuous enough to be beautiful
tipped over the vase of flowers that was their souls.
Every time I sinned it was as though a door opened
and tears of compassion fell on the grass.
And though guilt chased me out of heaven like a sword,
every time I sinned a door half opened and though men
found me ugly, the Angels found me beautiful.
                    – Melissanthi (Greek, 1910-1991)

2. Atonement

My reasons for it:

1. Men found me beautiful; angels found me ugly.

2. Every time I thought I might be beautiful, the angels said No.

3. Every time I opened the back door, my soul was there in the grass,
   chased out of heaven – where I was not found beautiful.

4. When men gave me flowers, the angels were in the vase, telling me
   I had sinned, my virtue was half full, and I was not beautiful.

5. Even though I offered them my guilt, they held me off with a
   door.

6. Every time I tipped to one side, my tears fell on an angel whose
   compassion blocked the door like a sword.

7. I want everyone to find me beautiful, even the angels.

3. Atonement

Though we may imagine Angels to be beautiful, there is evidence to the contrary. For example, the Angel who wielded his fiery sword when he chased our Parents out of Eden would have been hideous! Equally, Angels may be less compassionate than we surmise; surely we, too, would abandon the notion of virtue if we glimpsed the sins of Man every time we dared open our door. How ugly our world must seem, how full of guilt! The things Man creates – a picture, a vase, even a Cathedral – shall never be half as beautiful as a flower that springs from the grass, or the rain that is God's own tears. We must tip our hats to the Angels; only they know why they abide us.

Iconography

1. And the woman could not choose between the two men because one would have her and one would not, and one was true and one was a graven image.

2. She loved the image, for she created him from her own two minds, and he suited her.

3. She journeyed with him to the Far Sea and they stood, each turned away from the other, until the tide drew near to their feet.

4. The woman feared that the man would walk away, but the man feared not that she would walk away, for he was hers, and he thought not in her ways.

5. She said, 'You that I have made from my own self: walk away and we will not have been, or stay and let there be proof that we have loved, for soon the tide will conceal where we have stood.'

6. When the man was silent, the woman wept, for she perceived the silence and deemed him false. So she fell to her knees and prayed for testimony that the man was no shadow.

7. God sent an angel with a camera, but the man could not be captured. The angel said, 'That this man cannot be captured says not if he is false or a man. Return to the other man, for he gives you no such grief.' But the woman did not, though she knew she would grieve that which the tide would annul.

The Angels Wept

1. And it came to pass that the fountain of Bethesda flooded the land, for the angel stationed there wept through that long day.

2. A woman that waded among the multitudes held in her arms a box that she clasped like an infant.

3. She stopped at the foot of the angel, for she was tired. The angel said: 'Here was the path of the One Who Came Before You.'

4. The woman was startled, for she remembered that name, and knew that She once carried the box also. But the angel said no more and did not reveal that She had been a suicide and had left the box and her last quantity of gold with a plea that the Lord might find Her a successor.

5. But the woman who now held the box was wise, and though she knew not the One Who Came Before Her, she sensed her ghost upon her, and this ghost gave her fear, but also the ghost gave her strength.

6. She continued her path and faltered not, though among her trials were flood, sun, hills, cities, prison and sea.

7. And the Lord was pleased with her, though He did not condemn the One Who Came Before Her who died of her own hand, for He, like the angel, loved her with all His heart.

Here Comes the Bride

for Ivy and Davin Hatsengate

1. The bride held fast to her father's arm and walked with him to the altar, stopping at an old man who sat among the guests. She whispered to him through her veil, and the secret was heard by the woman who sat to his left side, and she wept to hear it.

2. On her lap sat a box, but the box was no gift for the bride and groom, but her own burden, which the Lord had allotted her.

3. Later at the feast, the wine did not run out and the music played until morning and all the villagers danced.

4. The woman laid her box on the grass and danced with the bride, for they had been girls together and loved one another. Distracted by the joy of the bride, and by her own joy also, she left the box unminded, dancing farther and farther from it.

5. When the dance was finished, the woman returned to the box with trepidation. And though it had not been moved, and nor had it been opened, it was lighter, and this puzzled her.

6. She recalled the secret that the bride had told the old man: 'God loves the woman who sits to your left, but I tell you and not her, for she will not believe it, and yet it must be known, but you must never speak of it.'

7. With guilt in her heart, she went to the old man to confess she knew the secret. But he was deaf and blind, and neither heard nor saw her.

III
Praise Him

I began to say the Jesus prayer in a whisper while I was sewing, and I liked it... in the end I got so used to the prayer that my tongue went on saying it by itself day and night.
                    – The Way of a Pilgrim

Who, if I cried out, would hear me among the angels' hierarchies?
                    – Rainer Maria Rilke

Angel with Book

for Jamie McKendrick

The angel's book is blue and dense and God knows the book,
which is nailed to the sky.

The angel is my friend and yet to say he has a good heart
is to be a poor physician,

for his wings are in his dodgy chest, speedy wings that beat
to a bad time.

His wings are all he's put away. His papers sit on rock and bog
and wind and desk,

on every noun in the world, even the flimsy nouns of the mind.

We all have dead friends, but he has more, and his big book
is the chronicle of harm.

Like his heart's flutter and his room's clutter, this book is his
                                        burden,
  and he has kept me out

using charm and guile and even lies, and I was grateful for my
                                        exclusion,
I was surprised.

To know the angel is to sense that you are gone. But to love him
                                        is to love
what isn't gone

like the world, the word and this angel who is fragile and who
                                        claims
no generosity, but is wrong.

Metrical Charm 10: For Loss of Cattle

from Old English

If you've been robbed, this is what you say. Say it immediately:

Just as it's well known to men
that Christ was born in Bethlehem,
make it known to all you see
a grievous wrong was done to me.
Per crucem Christi!

Then turn to the east, bow three times and say three times:
Crux Christi ab oriente reducat.

Then turn to the west, bow three times and say three times:
Crux Christi ab occidente reducat.

Then turn to the south, bow three times and say three times:
Crux Christi a meridie reducat.

Then turn to the north, bow three times and say three times:
Crux Christi abscondita sunt et inuenta est. Then:

Christ was tortured, crucified,
a truth his killers tried to hide.
Reveal this, then, to all you see:
a grievous crime was done to me.
Per crucem Christi.

Bright Day

Sometimes, but almost never,
when the light is Good
and the wind isn't wrong,
I say to the children, 'Look.'
And I make them stand, under God,
while the sky lords over their little minds
and I teach them to recognize
a 'God Day' when they see it.

But next time it happens,
they shout, 'It's a Mama Day!
She says she can see God.'
Every generation has its take on things.
My mother called it a Sunny Day.
Her mother called it a Day.

The Sun's Lecture Notes on Itself,
You and God

My sight is mindsight. Your sight is hindsight. His sight is insight.

*

When I rise I see the humans in the park. They walk whichever way
they walk. I see their progress in angles and vectors. Only God sees
where they are going.

*

The inner sun burns differently for each human. This includes ardour.

*

When you die and you think you see me, it is a version of me.
The woman who waits and holds out her hand: she too is a version.

*

Your pain will end whatever it is. That I can't say.

*

What you believed was great may have been nothing, and it was not
new. Nothing is new, but you knew that.

*

The answer most often is 'Yes.' but the 'yes' is mediated. As in 'Yes, but
not in the way you think.'

*

And you must live with discrepancy. We all live within a discrepancy.

*

The sky my colleague reminds you that the atmosphere is poison.
But he believes in free will and a daily change of eyesight.

*

Partial awareness is hardly a gift, but totality is worse. We look on you
and think this every day.

The Devil Will Find Work for Idle Minds

On the beach, every blonde is the girl
he'll leave me for.

The weather is fine;
happy families bob in the waves;
but everywhere is the pretty one, too.

A man shouts 'Melons and coconuts!'

I'm sure I see her on a towel,
pregnant with his child.

But she might be over there – ankle deep
in the sea with their twins,
smiling at the man who was mine.

The beach is a terrible place.

I can hear the fish say *carpe diem*,
the motto of the disloyal.

I have begun to pity the fashion models
of my generation
as the country celebrates their decline.

A second vendor sings 'Peaches!'

The sun projects itself on the world
and my husband adjusts the umbrella.

I wonder if I'll move to a Zen Buddhist abbey
to gain perspective after I'm left
for a sea-girl he can't fully possess.

If You Relive a Moment
You Cannot Outlive It

I have relived the same moment of happiness
so many times in my mind, it has taken a toll
on my physical health. As a consequence
of drinking the same glass of vodka year after
year, I've developed what the French call
crise de foie, which is apparently an early sign
of liver failure. We've had passion without
respite, which has been tiring,
not to mention all the babies produced –
and my weight gain has not been insubstantial.
I have suffered chronic headaches
due to the inhalation of cat piss wafting eternally
from the stairwell. I have gone deaf from
listening to blues and have also become depressed.
Is it possible to sue the past for medical damages?
I hope so because I have an ulcer
from the love I felt for you; and next week
I have an appointment with the cardiologist
because the prolonged stress and anxiety over what
you felt for me, which seemed to be nothing,
induced an arrhythmia so serious I have sometimes
required a crash cart. I should let the moment go
in the hopes my health improves, as one gives up
smoking or introduces a multivitamin,
but what's the point of living without any joy?

Assembly

for The Hall School

In lines the boys are perfect: what are they
in dreamy ranks, our babies or our men?
They pass us quickly when they hear *This way!*
and settle down in rows then rise to sing
Jesus lived here for men
strove and died, rose again
rules our hearts, now and then...
the voices die after they sing *amen*.

A teacher, newly wed, is smiling as
her pupil reads a poem and another
wins a cup for excellence in maths.
A boy behind a cello sees his mother
in the back, who wept at *none can see*
God above – and that concludes Assembly.

The Tall Thin Tenor

The tall thin tenor sings
The tall thin tenor sings to the young soprano
The young soprano sings the part of Poppea
The young woman Poppea has seduced the king
The tall thin tenor is king
The young soprano Poppea becomes the new young queen
The young soprano replaces the old queen Ottavia
The old queen Ottavia sings of replacement

The tall thin tenor sings over the soprano
The tall thin tenor sings over her to his small thin wife
His small thin wife holds a child in the stalls
His thin wife holds their quiet daughter
His small wife sings quietly to their daughter
The small wife is quiet when the queen sings

Legacy

If the Creation had been perfect,
and its symmetry had remained
unblemished, nothing we now know
would ever have been.
                    — Frank Close

The Lord said
Let there be
imperfection
and there was.
Let the left
testicle
hang lower
than the right.
Let the weight
of matter
equal that
of anti-
matter, but
let anti-
matter be
perfect, for
it is my
opposite.
Let me be
good and not
God, or God
and not good.
And let the
universe
have light/dark
heaven/earth
man/woman
so it can
give it all

back to me
in reverse:
woman/man,
earth/heaven
and light, but
let the world
keep the dark,
for the dark
void has no
counterpart
for nothing
can have one
exactly
nothing but
the lord God
before you.

Number Plate Bible

B49 NSD
Banished

A4L BOT
Animal Boat

MO5E SRS
Moses Stutters

AB24 ABM
Absalom, Absalom

YM3 J08
Why Me, Said Job

BL77 MEE
Blessed Are the Meek

M15 H1R
Mary's Hair

JE56 WPT
Jesus Wept

ST2 PUL
St. Paul

TR6 66PS
Trumpets

Street Sweeper

God scatters where he eats.
The sweeper wheels his cart to what falls.

The broom assembles a pile.
The wind dismantles the pile.

God is the messy wind. The pile
is the mouthpiece of the wind.

Sometimes the wind is bluster.
Sometimes the wind is a mute.

There is the God who listens.
There is the God who speaks.

The God who listens is a gentle liar.
The God who speaks is laconic and hard.

I ask if I'm loved.
He points to the graveyard his garden abuts.

I clutch his hair. I say *Am I loved?*
He claims his love for me is deep

but zealless. Over the garden wall,
the God who listens, the neighbour,

smiles when I ask if I am loved.
He points to the God across the wall,

the first God, the God I just left,
as if to say *God loves you.*

Sometimes he speaks through his dog.
Sometimes he doesn't speak.

If his mother tongue were 'dog'
or 'frog' or 'wind' or 'rubbish'

could I learn that language
and hear that I was loved?

Or would the answer
be something I couldn't hear.

The Periodic Table won't revoke
what it has put in the world –

earth metals, non–metals, catalysts.
It is God's slovenly generosity

and is difficult to gather,
as the street sweeper knows,

as the wind knows, as I know, and God knows.
The sweeper smiles at me lovingly

like the silent god,
the one with the message I cannot hear.

Acknowledgements

Acknowledgement is due to the editors of the following periodicals, anthologies and websites in which many of these poems first appeared:

Agenda, Best American Poetry (website), *Dark Matter: Poems of Space* (ed. Maurice Riordan and Jocelyn Bell-Burnell, Gulbenkian Foundation, 2008), *The Harvard Review, The Guardian* (website), *Green Mountains Review, Limelight, Lung Jazz* (ed. Todd Swift and Kim Lockwood, Cinnamon Press, 2012), *Magma, Modern Poetry in Translation, New Welsh Review, nthposition, Oxford Poets 2010: An Anthology* (ed.David Constantine, Robyn Marsack and Bernard O'Donoghue, Carcanet), *The Word Exchange* (ed. Greg Delanty and Michael Matto, WW Norton, 2009), *Ploughshares, Poetry London, Poetry Review, Poetry Calendar* (Alhambra Press 2008, 2009, 2010), *Slate, The Spectator, Tokens for the Foundlings* (ed. Tony Curtis, Seren, 2012), and *The Word Exchange* (ed. Greg Delanty and Michael Matto, W.W. Norton, 2009.

'Angel with Book' (originally titled 'Angel with Big Book') received a Pushcart Prize and appeared in *The Pushcart Prize Anthology XXXIII*. 'What Will Happen to the Neighbours When the Earth Floods?' was included in *Best British Poetry 2012* (ed. Roddy Lumsden and Sasha Dugdale, Salt Publishing).

'Darling Will You Please Pick up those Books' and 'This Is a Confessional Poem' were commended in the International Troubadour Poetry Competition (2008 and 2009).

'What Will Happen to the Neighbours When the Earth Floods?' is dedicated to Ben and Rachel Elwes.

I am grateful for residencies at Yaddo and the Hawthornden Castle, where many of these poems were written.

Warm thanks are due to Jamie McKendrick, Kathryn Simmonds; the Lamb group, 2006-2010; Frank Close (Professor of Physics, Oxford) for a 3-hour conversation about the Higgs Boson and other aspects of particle physics that yielded two poems in this collection, 'Why' and 'Legacy'; Mimi Khalvati for her Versification class at the Poetry School; Herman, Mathijs and Cosima Deetman; Amy Wack and staff at Seren; and especially Maurice Riordan.

About the Author

Kathryn Maris is a poet from New York City. She attended Columbia University where she studied with Kenneth Koch, and has an MA from Boston University, where among her teachers were Robert Pinsky, Derek Walcott and Geoffrey Hill. She has published poems in *The Spectator, Poetry Review, The Harvard Review, Modern Poetry in Translation, Poetry, Slate* and several anthologies including *Best British Poetry* and *Oxford Poets 2010.* Among her awards are an Academy of American Poets University & College Prize, a Pushcart Prize, and fellowships from the Fine Arts Work Center in Provincetown, Yaddo, and the Hawthornden Castle. Her first collection, *The Book of Jobs*, was published in the US by Four Way Books in 2006. She has taught creative writing at Boston University, the Gotham Writers Workshop, Kingston University and, currently, at Morley College and the Poetry School in London. She also writes essays and reviews for British and American periodicals.